Kobe Bryant

By Jeff Savage

AMAZING
ATHLETES

LERNER**SPORTS** /**Minneapolis**

This book is available in two editions:
Library binding by LernerSports
Soft cover by First Avenue Editions
Imprints of Lerner Publishing Group
241 First Avenue North
Minneapolis, MN 55401 U.S.A.

Website address: www.lernerbooks.com

Library of Congress Cataloging-in-Publication Data

Savage, Jeff, 1961–
      Kobe Bryant / by Jeff Savage.
         p.   cm. — (Amazing athletes)
      Summary: Introduces the life and accomplishments of basketball guard Kobe Bryant, whose high scoring game helped bring the Los Angeles Lakers three straight world championships.
      Includes bibliographical references and index.
      ISBN: 0–8225–1300–5 (lib. bdg. : alk. paper)
      ISBN: 0–8225–9849–3 (pbk. : alk. paper)
      1. Bryant, Kobe, 1978—Juvenile literature. 2. Basketball players—United States—Biography—Juvenile literature. 3. Los Angeles Lakers (Basketball team)—Juvenile literature. [1. Bryant, Kobe, 1978– 2. Basketball players. 3. African Americans—Biography.] I. Title. II. Series.
      GV884.B794 S27 2003
      796.323'092—dc21   2002015764

Manufactured in the United States of America
1 2 3 4 5 6 – DP – 08 07 06 05 04 03

TABLE OF CONTENTS

Netting a Title	4
A Broad Education	9
High School Star	13
A Kid in a Man's Game	19
A Shooting Star	24
Selected Career Highlights	29
Glossary	29
Further Reading & Websites	31
Index	32

In 2002, Kobe and his teammates were in the hunt for a third NBA Championship.

NETTING A TITLE

Kobe Bryant's team, the Los Angeles Lakers, needed to score. They were playing in the 2002 National Basketball Association (NBA) Championship against the New Jersey Nets.

The Lakers had led most of the game. But the Nets had scored eleven straight points to take the lead early in the final quarter. Kobe passed the ball inside to Shaquille O'Neal. Shaq passed it right back to Kobe, who was standing behind the three-point line. Kobe caught the pass and sailed the ball toward the hoop. It swished through the net for three points. The score was tied, 87–87.

Kobe's shooting skills helped the Lakers win the title in the final quarter.

Kobe tries to drive around the Nets' Kenyon Martin.

Los Angeles was trying to win its fourth straight game against the Nets. A victory would give the Lakers their third NBA title in a row. Kobe was a big reason why the Lakers were so good. Many people consider Kobe to be the greatest basketball player in the world.

A clutch player plays best at the end of a close game. Some people believe Kobe has become one of the NBA's best clutch players.

As the fourth-quarter clock wound down, the Lakers started to take control of the game. Kobe was the key. The Nets tried to stop him, but Kobe scored eleven of his twenty-five points in the final quarter. With four minutes left, he got past two defenders and floated into the **lane** for a short **jump shot.**

Kobe goes to the basket in the final minutes of the fourth game.

The shot gave the Lakers a 100–93 lead. The Nets couldn't catch up. The Lakers won the game, 113–107. Afterward, Kobe and his teammates celebrated their third straight world championship.

Kobe holds up the trophy for the Lakers winning their third championship. His teammate Shaquille O'Neal *(right)* holds the trophy as the championship's most valuable player.

As a kid, Kobe watched his dad, Joe "Jellybean" Bryant, play professional basketball for the Philadelphia 76ers.

A BROAD EDUCATION

Kobe Bryant learned the sport of basketball as a young boy. Kobe's father, Joe, played sixteen years as a professional, eight in the NBA. Joe's nickname was "Jellybean," because a fan once gave him jelly beans.

Kobe was born August 23, 1978, into a close family. His mother, Pam, and his older sisters, Sharia and Shaya, are among his most supportive fans.

When Kobe was three, he began watching his father play basketball on television. Kobe put his little hoop next to the TV and watched his father shoot the basketball. Then Kobe would shoot his foam basketball at his hoop, pretending to be just like dad. In 1984, Kobe's father left the NBA to join a professional league in Europe. Kobe packed his basketball and hoop and his other belongings and moved with his family to Italy.

Kobe's middle name is Bean, which is short for "Jellybean."

Kobe already spoke English, of course. He learned to speak Italian in school. At home, he

The Bryant family lived in Pistoia, Italy, while Joe was playing for the European leagues. During his stay, Kobe practiced his basketball skills.

practiced new Italian words with his sisters at the kitchen table.

Kobe also practiced basketball. He would **dribble** and shoot every day at the school playground. But in Europe, soccer is much more popular than basketball. So, when the other children arrived with a soccer ball, Kobe had to put his basketball away.

Kobe has said his parents encouraged him to be an individual. "They taught me that there would be criticisms. . . , but you've just got to do what you think is right."

When Kobe was eight, he started going to his father's pro basketball practices. Kobe sometimes practiced with the team. He learned to make smart passes and be a good teammate. The Italian players had fun playing with Kobe.

In 1991, when Kobe was thirteen, he and his family returned to the United States. They lived near Philadelphia, Pennsylvania. Kobe spoke proper English, which he had learned from textbooks. Many American boys spoke **slang.** It was difficult for Kobe to understand their words. He was even teased. Playing basketball helped Kobe make friends.

By the time Kobe was at Lower Merion High School, his basketball skills were already well above those of his classmates.

HIGH SCHOOL STAR

Kobe studied hard and earned good grades during his four years at Lower Merion High School in Pennsylvania. He was an instant star for the school basketball team, the Aces.

Kobe wowed crowds with his quickness, strength, and drive to get the ball to the basket.

In one game, he had the flu but played anyway and led the Aces to a victory. In another, he made nine of ten second-half shots to pull off an amazing comeback win. He could play any position, and he mostly played **point guard** so that he could dribble the ball for his team.

Kobe's father once played for the NBA's Philadelphia 76ers. In 1994, Joe Bryant asked the 76ers coach to allow Kobe to practice with the team. The coach kindly agreed. Kobe was just sixteen, but he was able to keep up with the pro players. In fact, sometimes he was the best player on the court.

The Philadelphia 76ers (here playing against the Washington Bullets, later Wizards) allowed Kobe to practice with them in the mid-1990s. Kobe was still in high school!

Kobe led his Lower Merion team to the 1996 state championship.

Michael Jordan is widely thought to be the greatest basketball player ever. Even in high school, though, people whispered that Kobe might someday become as great as Jordan.

As a senior in high school, Kobe averaged thirty-one points, twelve **rebounds,** and seven **assists** per game. He led Lower Merion to a 31–3 record and the Pennsylvania state title. He finished his four years of high school as the leading scorer in southern Pennsylvania history, breaking the 1950s record of the great Wilt Chamberlain.

Wilt Chamberlain shows off his big hands. He was a star basketball player in high school, college, and the NBA.

Colleges around the country invited Kobe to play for their basketball team. Kobe had good grades and was talented enough to go to the college of his choice. But Kobe announced that he was available for the 1996 NBA **draft.** Every summer, all the pro teams take turns picking two promising players each. Most of the players chosen have finished college. Kobe was about to become just the seventh player in thirty years to go straight from high school to the NBA.

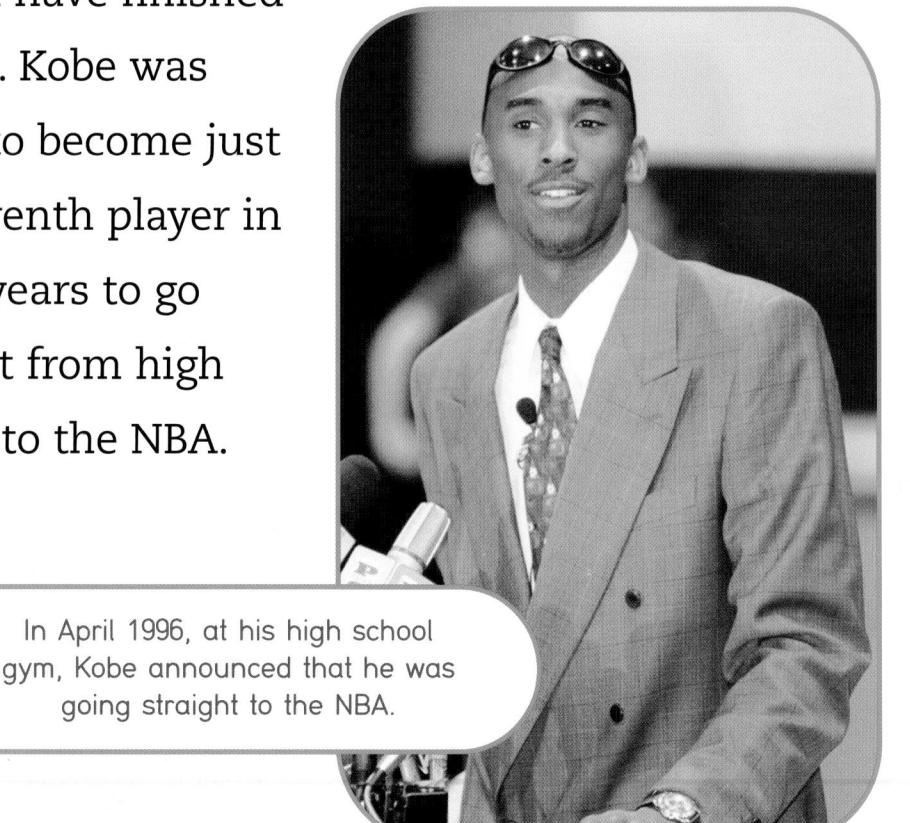

In April 1996, at his high school gym, Kobe announced that he was going straight to the NBA.

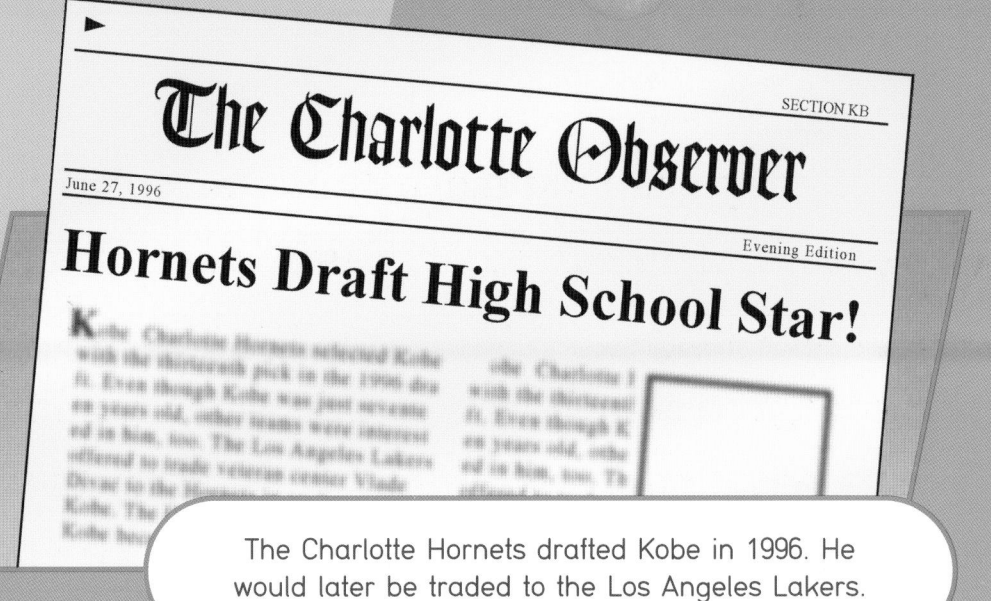

SECTION KB

June 27, 1996

Evening Edition

The Charlotte Observer

Hornets Draft High School Star!

The Charlotte Hornets drafted Kobe in 1996. He would later be traded to the Los Angeles Lakers.

A KID IN A MAN'S GAME

The Charlotte Hornets selected Kobe with the thirteenth pick in the 1996 draft. Even though Kobe was just seventeen years old, other teams were interested in him, too.

The Los Angeles Lakers offered to trade **veteran** center Vlade Divac to the Hornets in exchange for Kobe. The Hornets accepted the offer. Kobe became a member of the Lakers.

Kobe signed a three-year **contract** with the Lakers for $3.5 million. Kobe and his family moved west to Los Angeles. With some of the money, Kobe bought a big house in a wealthy area. The house was roomy enough for the family to live together. Kobe's bedroom overlooked the Pacific Ocean and downtown Los Angeles.

After the trade, Kobe moved to Los Angeles. He enjoyed hanging out with his family and friends in his new house.

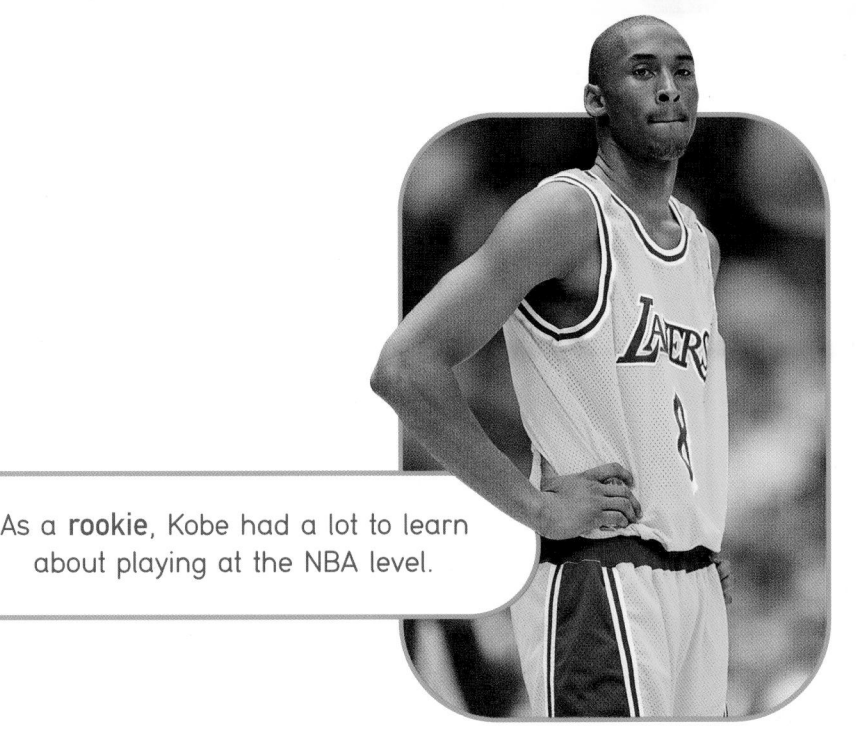

As a **rookie**, Kobe had a lot to learn about playing at the NBA level.

Kobe had grown to six feet seven inches. He could shoot, pass, dribble, and rebound well enough to play any position. He usually played guard.

Kobe was barely eighteen years old when he became the youngest player ever to play in an NBA game. Against the Minnesota Timberwolves, Kobe played six minutes of the game. He missed one shot, made one rebound, and had one **block.**

Crowds at the All-Star Game in early 1997 cheered Kobe's slam dunks. He won the annual contest.

Kobe learned plenty as a rookie, and he began to play more minutes each game. His favorite part of the season was the All-Star Game. He won the slam dunk contest.

Kobe was much younger than his teammates, and it wasn't always easy for him.

After games, Kobe's teammates would go out to nightclubs, while Kobe would go home. In his free time, he'd hang out with his sisters.

Throughout all his early success, Kobe remained very close to his family. Here, he goes out on the town with his sister Sharia.

Kobe played with and got advice from Michael Jordan at the 1998 All-Star Game.

A SHOOTING STAR

Kobe continued to practice and improve. He wasn't a **starter** on the Lakers yet, so it was shocking that one of his first NBA starts came in the 1998 NBA All-Star Game. Fans across the country had voted to see Kobe play. He even got to play with the great Michael Jordan.

Kobe put on quite a show at the All-Star Game. He scored a team-high eighteen points with a variety of acrobatic shots. Kobe became a starter on the Lakers soon after.

Kobe quickly became a star. He was scoring twenty points or more in games. He was making smart passes to his teammates and playing sticky defense.

Kobe's hard work paid off in his second season. The Lakers made him a starter after the All-Star Game.

In June 2002, Kobe held up three fingers to show that the Lakers had won their third straight NBA Championship.

At first, Kobe and center Shaquille O'Neal tended to compete with one another more than they helped each other on the court. Eventually, though, they developed into a dynamic duo. The Lakers beat the Indiana Pacers in the 2000 NBA Finals to win the title. They won their second straight world championship in 2001 by defeating the Philadelphia 76ers. Their third straight title in 2002 was a 4–0 defeat of the New Jersey Nets.

Kobe had a string of high-scoring games in the 2002–2003 season. His high scoring helped get the Lakers to the **postseason.** This time, though, the team didn't make it to the finals.

Kobe has become very popular with fans. His number 8 jersey outsells every other Lakers' number, even Shaquille O'Neal's number 34.

By the end of this game against the Washington Wizards, Kobe had scored fifty-five points.

Kobe and his wife, Vanessa *(seated beside Kobe)*, enjoy going to sports and entertainment events whenever they can.

Kobe continues to grow in new ways. He married Vanessa Laine in 2001, and their first child was born in 2003. When Kobe isn't spending time with his family, he is working hard on his game. "I want to be," he says, "the best player who ever set foot on a basketball court."

Selected Career Highlights

2002–2003 named to the All-NBA First Team
received most votes in NBA All-Star ballot
made record-breaking twelve three-pointers in
a single game
became youngest player in NBA history to reach
10,000 points for his career

2001–2002 named to the All-NBA First Team
as member of the Lakers, won his third NBA
Championship

2000–2001 named to the All-NBA Second Team
as member of the Lakers, won his second NBA
Championship

1999–2000 named to the All-NBA Second Team
as member of the Lakers, won his first
NBA Championship

1998–1999 named to the All-NBA Third Team

1997–1998 became the youngest player ever to
start in the NBA All-Star Game

1996–1997 became the youngest player ever to play in an NBA game
won the NBA slam dunk contest at the All-Star Game
set the NBA All-Star Rookie Game scoring record with thirty-
one points
became the youngest player to appear in an NBA game
named National High School Player of the Year

Glossary

assist: a pass to a teammate that allows that teammate to score

block: stopping an opponent's shot from going in the hoop by striking the ball

contract: a written deal signed by a player and his or her team. The player agrees to play for the team for a stated number of years. The team agrees to pay the player a stated amount of money.

draft: a yearly event in which all professional teams in a sport are given the chance to pick new players from a selected group. Most of the players in the group have played their sport in college.

dribble: the continuous bouncing of the ball, using one hand

inside: the area near or underneath the basketball hoop

jump shot: a shot of any length in which a player jumps in the air before shooting the ball over a defender

lane: an area at the end of the basketball court underneath each basket

pass: to throw or bounce the basketball to a teammate in order to move the ball closer to the basket

point guard: a player on a basketball team whose chief role is to run the offense, when the team has the ball

postseason: the games played after the regular season ends

quarter: one of four periods in a basketball game

rebound: to catch the ball off the hoop or the backboard after a missed shot

rookie: a player who is playing his or her first season

slang: words that are playful or odd, but not proper grammar

starter: a person who is named to play from the beginning of the game

three-point line: a curved line, or arc, on the floor at each end of the court. Shots made from outside this line are worth three points.

veteran: a player who has played more than one season. A player is usually called a veteran after he or she has played several seasons.

Further Reading & Websites

Kirkpatrick, Rob. *Kobe Bryant: Slam Dunk Champion.* New York: Powerkids Press, 2000.

Macnow, Glen. *Sports Great Kobe Bryant.* Berkeley Heights, NJ: Enslow Publishers, 2000.

Savage, Jeff. *Kobe Bryant: Basketball Big Shot.* Minneapolis, MN: LernerSports, 2001.

Stewart, Mark. *Kobe Bryant: Hard to the Hoop.* Brookfield, CT: The Millbrook Press, 2000.

Stout, Glenn. *On the Court With . . . Kobe Bryant.* New York: Little Brown & Co., 2001.

Torres, John Albert. *Kobe Bryant.* Bear, DE: Mitchell Lane Publishers, 2000.

Los Angeles Lakers Website
<http://www.nba.com/lakers>
The official website of the Lakers includes team schedules, late-breaking news, profiles of past and present players, and much more.

Official NBA Website
<http://www.nba.com>
A website developed by the National Basketball Association (NBA) that provides fans with recent news stories, statistics, biographies of players and coaches, and information about games.

Sports Illustrated for Kids
<http://www.sikids.com>
The *Sports Illustrated for Kids* website that covers all sports, including basketball.

Index

Aces, the, 13, 14
All-Star Game, 22, 24–25

Bryant, Joe "Jellybean," 9, 10, 12
Bryant, Kobe, childhood of, 9–17;
    early talent of, 9, 12, 13, 14–17;
    and family, 9, 10, 11, 20, 23, 28;
    and life in Italy, 10–12; as a
    professional, 4–8, 18–21, 24–27;
    as a rookie, 21–23; and school,
    10–18
Bryant, Pam, 10
Bryant, Sharia, 10, 23
Bryant, Shaya, 10

Chamberlain, Wilt, 17
Charlotte Hornets, 19

Divac, Vlade, 19

Indiana Pacers, 26
Italy, 10, 11, 12

Jordan, Michael, 16, 24

Laine, Vanessa, 28
Los Angeles, California, 20
Los Angeles Lakers, 4, 5, 6, 19–20,
    24–25, 26, 27
Lower Merion High School, 13, 14,
    16, 17

Martin, Kenyon, 6
Minnesota Timberwolves, 21

National Basketball Association
    (NBA), 4, 6, 9, 10, 15, 17, 18, 21,
    24
NBA Championship, 4–8, 26
NBA draft, 18–19
New Jersey Nets, 4–8, 26

O'Neal, Shaquille, 5, 8, 26, 27

Pennsylvania, 13, 17
Philadephia, Pennsylvania, 12
Philadelphia 76ers, 9, 15, 26
Pistoia, Italy, 11

Washington Wizards, 15, 27

Photo Acknowledgments

Photographs are used with permission of: AP/Wide World Photos, pp. 4, 7,
8, 18, 27, 28; © Icon SMI, p. 5; © Reuters NewMedia Inc./CORBIS, pp. 6, 29;
Vicki Valerio, *Philadelphia Inquirer*, p. 9; © Michael Freeman/CORBIS, p. 11; ©
Jay Gorodetzer, pp. 13, 14, 16; Andrea Mihalik, *Philadelphia Daily News*, p. 15;
© Bettmann/CORBIS, p. 17; Bill Hauser, p. 19; © Neal Preston/CORBIS, p. 20;
© David Taylor/Getty Images, p. 21; © Brian Bahr/Getty Images, p. 22; © Lisa
Rose/Globe Photos, Inc., p. 23; © AFP/CORBIS, pp. 24, 26; SportsChrome
East/West, Michael Zito, p. 25.

Cover: © Reuters NewMedia Inc./CORBIS.